Let the Scaffolding Collapse

poems by

Renee Podunovich

Finishing Line Press

Georgetown, Kentucky

Let the Scaffolding Collapse

ACKNOWLEDGMENTS

I would like to thank the following journals for their publication of individual poems in previous versions:

"Behind the Wind", FutureCycle Poetry, 2011.
"Restless", FutureCycle Poetry, 2011, nominated for Pushcart poetry prize in 2011.
"This Poem is Not About Me", RATTLE, #34, Winter, 2010.
"It Makes All the Difference", Caper Literary Journal, Winter, 2010 (honorable mention for Maravillosa Magical Realism contest).
"Bondage", Right Hand Pointing, Issue 35, 2010.
"Pulse", White Whale Review, Issue 2.2, 2010.
"Designed to Catch The Enormous", White Whale Review, Issue 2.2, 2010.
"I Loved Your Appendix", Boston Literary Magazine, Summer, 2010, nominated for the Pushcart poetry prize in 2010.
"Swirls All", The View From Here, Issue 24, May, 2010.

Editor: Christen Kincaid

Cover Photo: McCarson L. Jones

Author Photo: Mark Montgomery

Cover Design: Christen Kincaid

Printed in the USA on acid-free paper.
Order online: www.finishinglinepress.com
also available on amazon.com

Author inquiries and mail orders:
Finishing Line Press
P. O. Box 1626
Georgetown, Kentucky 40324
U. S. A.

TABLE OF CONTENTS

I Loved Your Appendix

They took it.
pink and yellow tissue,
tender apricot flesh,
an add-on to you,
    an inconsequential appendage,
    a mere flap of skin, useless.
Your bare abdomen.
a summer meadow dotted with the yellow
Shasta Daisies of my kisses.
    and small incisions
    red and opening.
For one instant I saw inside
    the envelope of your skin.
skin like vellum, smooth, silk, soft leather
supple from years of hard work.
    warm, scented like cardamom,
    persimmons, wood smoke, just moist like
grape leaves folded over hidden
and fragile innards.
They said you won't miss it
but now I have less of you,
    an appendix less, an ounce less,
as brief as a moment,
a blink while stargazing.
Yet someday
one of us will pass on,
    not impalpable
    but the whole body,
an ocean of passion become motionless,
the shell of us left for the other to hold to the ear,
listening for the roar of the sea,
    for memories that bubble to the surface
    from the blackness of canyons and crevices
in the deep.
The extravagance of having extra organs.
This flesh, breath, death.
Delicate, so
    delicate.

This Poem Is Not About Me

Because not everything I write is
about myself. I used the word "she"
not "me". "he" not "you". this is
fiction. made up. which is different
than fantasy. that myopia
that funnels the infinite potential of awareness
through a skinny garden hose
into a blow-up kiddie pool
in a tiny backyard of the mind.
one thought. only one. over and over.
it's about you. I mean him. I mean she
always thinks about him.
and when that pool gets too full it floods.
runs over. moodiness. not satisfied with things
as they are. she likes to swim with a pair of fantasy
goggles. everything takes on that tinge. that blur.
but she always tires eventually of bathing her adult
body in that ridiculous little pool. annoyed
that her limbs hang over the sides. her weight
pulling them flat so the water escapes
onto the grass. that's when she takes
those goggles off. and things are
just like this. just now.
she is suddenly a huge deity. Kwan Yin.
hovering above the entire ocean. light
reflects on its surfaces. buoyed by waves
and that need. that longing. those fabrications
are now a dime that fell out of someone's
swimming trunks. just like that.
surfs and settles in the sand. now forgotten.
and the water is so large. unimaginable.
and remember. I was just a swimmer nearby.
it didn't happen to me.

Restless

His teeth sink into her pillow.
every night he dreams that he is an appliance
that is coming unplugged and in the free fall
feeling of that dislocation,
he startles awake.
to discover that he has grabbed
the nearest soft thing he can find
and has her pillow clenched in his mouth
and if he removes it he might scream.
he mutters in his sleep:
not integrated. I'm a clock radio.
brisket. army truck. get out.

they eat breakfast quietly.
he can't remember the nightmares
exactly, but they haunt him
and so he eats abnormal amounts of
toast and eggs. she doesn't know
what to say to him
about these nocturnal assertions.
can't bear to tell him that in fact
it is she who shoves the pillow
toward his gaping mouth to appease
the molars and incisors and canines
and avoid the possibility that he might
instead devour her. without even
waking up. would see her in the morning
just a skeleton. picked clean.
thin and white and perfectly
at rest.

Bondage

A plate of spaetzel.
her brain chemistry. the booze. her moods.
she's like a grab bag.
don't know what you'll get.
the paper crinkles
as you fondle what is hidden
inside. that's the best part.
the grab. so why open it?
it's not gravity. not destiny.
there's something else behind the pull.
she's sticky like her lip gloss.
if someone kissed her right now
their lips would be stuck to hers
for all eternity.

Unraveled

Her life is a ball of yarn
that might have been perfectly round to begin with,
but now is coming unwound.
loose filaments trail behind her.
sometimes she holds the end of the string
and the ball rolls away and away.
until it is out of sight and if it is yellow
or orange, it becomes the sun,
straddling the horizon at sunset.
she doesn't worry about it though.
it's like an endless yarn supply. her life.
the ball never gets smaller or if it does
there is always another skein.
she doesn't knit or crochet either.

you might feel like you want to gather
all of this up. untangle any knots. start creating
an orderly situation. where everything rolls up
neatly. where things get put into place.
settled. situated. just so.
but that is your desire. not hers.
she doesn't mind the stray threads.
she didn't ask you to stitch it all together.
she doesn't want to borrow the beautiful
hand-woven basket in which you organize your yarn.

she wants to be un-tethered. a kite string
that breaks and floats high. she wants
to sleep with the doors open. let the wind
blow in and out easily all night long.
she leaves bits of lint on your sweater
every time you see her.
and you don't brush it off.

Falling Down the Chimney

It's hard to admit that she isn't a nice person
anymore. that she is totally sick of doing everything
right. getting it all perfect. putting on a costume
and announcing, *I'm in total control of my life
and everything is great!*
if she stays busy she can ignore
that she is starting to think
that all of this thinking is just tangled and knotted up thoughts.
maybe she's caught in them
like when someone catches their big toe
in one of those rope hammocks that aren't comfortable.
nothing worse than bad design.
and if there is no belief in anything, then what?
the hollow pull of emptiness.
like falling down the chimney.
fear of failure. exhaustion. losing ground.
misplaced meaning. trying to find it every place
            it surely is not:
            a bottle of red wine (or white),
            calling old flames, another pair
of shoes (she needs them for work).
on a really bad day, she screams into her cell phone
            (at a coworker? an ex?)
she paces frantically up and down the hallway.
oblivious.
everyone can hear her.
the secretary gently motions her inside.
looks apologetic as she closes the door.
contains the tantrum.
this is what it looks like when the pressure blows
            and everyone sees. like sushi.
entirely raw. fascinating and revolting.
and what can you do except act as if you aren't looking.
didn't notice that the seams of her suit are near bursting
and underneath the stage make-up—
            fear of falling.
            of disappearing down the flue.

Never Say Later

He should never say, *We'll talk later, darling.*
when what he really wants to say to her is,
You are driving me crazy and I want to shoo you
the way I want DEET to keep the mosquitoes
from the tender flesh of my inner thighs.

he can't take it anymore.
all of her needs like straws and he's some liquid
and there's only one free re-fill at this place
but she wants another one.
she is a glue stick. flattening
and glue-sticking him to the pages of her journal,
drawing devil horns or halos depending
on her mood that day.
he says, *Later, later, later.*
but what he hopes is to collapse into himself.
the place where no one gets in.
where he can toss out scribbles
on wadded scraps of paper,
periodically,
as a form of communication.
she opens them eagerly.
with invisible ink he writes:
> place the empty barrel of me
> under rain gutters.
> let me sit quietly through this storm,
> filling. and when I spill over,
> then.
> that's when.

Indra's Net of Jewels

He is a guy who doesn't respond.
but everyone wants to talk to him.
and the more he says nothing, the more they say.
and the more they say the heavier he becomes
as if their words stick in him like fish in a net
and he can't get them out.
To say something like
the heat is a beautiful jewel
that sparkles on the summer river
could drown him. it's too much.

everyone has to deal with their own
intensity. find a way to fashion
betrayal and heartbreak and hard knocks
into a dory that floats the self
across the ocean of immense unknowing.
His boat has a hole that seems bottomless
and no amount of anything can patch it.

Eventually everyone stops talking.
lets him sink.
hopes that Indra's net of jewels hovers
somewhere in those deep waters
and somehow, sometime, maybe this time
it will catch him
long enough to gather force and swim.
hard to the surface and in a huge gasp
decide to keep breathing. this air that is both
deliciously fresh and terribly sorrowful.
and not slip through the webbing
into that silent somewhere
that no one can follow.

She is a Magnet for Narcissists

She seems so assertive and sure of herself.
for instance, she just returned a too bitter,
too strong iced coffee. and then another.
actually walked up to the counter and said,
This is bad. Really bad. twice.
but now she's become confused.
thinks maybe that was rude.
wonders if she hurt the barista's feelings.
wasted resources. made a scene. caused a hassle.
and that confusion bears down
like a French press on her heart.
the one she hides away
so that no one notices it's amber pulse.
and steps on it. accidentally.
or worse, on purpose.
she thinks maybe he steps on it
on purpose. a sadistic pleasure.
he finds that heartbeat when no one else can.
when it is weak and forgotten. even to her.
he captures it gently.
but always gets rough. like someone grabbing
a dog by the collar and scolding it. too harshly.
and that tugging starts to hurt. it's humiliating.
that's when she starts to get a little mad.
starts to remember herself as her pulse quickens,
in fact, races
and she wants to stand up for that dog.
She might just tell him sometime.
        soon.
that he is bad for her.
really bad.

Single Male Friends

She keeps them like crickets in wicker cages.
like in Asian fairy tales. for good luck
and the soothing sound of their chirping.
they come with directions:
      never keep more than one male in the same cricket house.
      they are very territorial and will probably
      end up killing one another.
      the males sing (mostly at night) to attract the females
      and to scare off the other males.
she's learned to have one at a time.
she's sure he chirps just to make her happy.
on long layovers, in lonely hotel rooms
or when eating alone at the bar,
he's always available to text or chat.
she can move him where ever she wants.
she could take him to work with her and set him on her desk.
but he might distract her coworkers.
so in the mornings, before she leaves,
she sets him on her dresser in the bedroom.
she closes the bedroom door and leaves a note on it
so her husband won't open it and let the cat in.
the cat would find the cricket,
bat him around with her paws for several hours,
torture him fatally, then eat half of him,
leaving the rest of his mangled body on her rug.
then she would have nothing but the empty wicker cage
and all of the problems his constant chirping disguised.
now pounding her ears with their deafening presence.
she would have to get expensive new headphones.
the good kind. noise canceling. the relief
of that white noise would wrap around her
so she could continue to avoid
contact with chaos and try to rest
amid the restlessness awhile.

It Makes All the Difference

She is lounging on a pool float
but not swimming.
no one has used that long-handled net scoop
and the dead bugs are floating
      like show girls in leotards
      fallen from their trapeze,
now suspended by a safety net of green murk.
she skims her fingers across the surface
and the algae hangs there
      like a lover's hair,
slowly slides off and flies
      like a private jet
as she hurtles it at the wall of the courtyard.
it splats. stays stuck to the stucco.
no one joins her pool party.
they smile sweetly from the sides.
check their watches. make excuses:
the kids. a meeting. forgot a suit.
I have an extra Speedo, she offers,
the cabana boy will fetch it for you.
I'm in the weeds at work, he says,
straightening his tie nervously,
then waves a sheepish goodbye and hurries away.
She flings a clump of slimy algae
at the back of his head
      like a grenade.
      she misses. oh well.
she adjusts her straw hat and sunglasses.
sips her iced tea. points her pedicured toes
and dips them gingerly into the muck.
she prepares for a refreshing plunge
by closing her eyes. it makes all the difference
to close her eyes.

So Easily They Linger

All day long things have been turning.
inside out. first a $5 umbrella he purchased for me
from the vendor on the sidewalk in front of the Met,
now inverted with spine and ribs torqued aggressively
in the wrong direction. just like my words.
how they escaped from my mouth
by some force as transitory
yet insistent as the wind.
immediately I want to take them back.
see how they have flattened him
and for most of the day we are figures
in a Persian miniature.
even at lunch in the museum café,
I try to fork those transgressions back in
with bites of brie, walnuts and baby greens.
but cruel words don't go away so easily. they linger
and later appear in the Oceana exhibit
as body masks from New Guinea.
their giant eyes see what is hidden.
their leathery lips beckon shadow selves to light.
their woven fibers and sago palm leaves flail
in every direction and they don't behave
like a person normally would. or should.

I wonder what it would be like
to put them on.
wave our arms. say those terrible things
that we aren't supposed to say.
a tsunami of repressed sentiments
would fill the quiet exhibit space. wreck
everything for awhile,
making space for possibilities
before disappearing into silence.

and when we take the wild masks off,
we will be just two people visiting the museum.
getting along fine.

Grip

Letting go of his hand,
his fingers linger in the soft concave
of her palm.
at any moment during the separation
of skin against skin,
she could close her grip again
around the comfort of his warm pulse.
but she lets go of grasping for his attention,
lets his hand become a butterfly,
    his fingers five wings
    that belong only to him,
    mutable and fluid
    now lifted by wind,
shifted into flight,
taking him to higher ground.
    that sense of impossibility
    to be able to change
drives him to distractions
that are like unopened petals
or already spent blossoms.
    He claps his hands.
    the sharp sound like
    his heart exploding.
He is ready to elevate,
let the unimagined through the door
that he always keeps closed,
now blown open an inch
by the force of having two
free hands.

Behind the Wind

It seems like I've known him
forever. the years are stacked up like pancakes
and the stack has become so tall that the ones
on the bottom can't even be seen anymore.
are just vague, reconstructed or falsified memories.
but they are there at the bottom of the pile
holding the whole thing up.
that's how long I've known him.
but today at the beach. seeing him from behind.
the wind sifted through his graying hair.
it appears something magnificent is moving
and blowing him along the shore.
he leans over. gathering. looking.
paying attention to the world
and the moment before him
and I wonder, *Who is this man?*
the one running up smiling.
Look at these, he says of a handful of shells.
broken. fragments. remains. rubble mostly.
some are whole and a few are quite extraordinary.
but he is holding them like they are the most amazing
gift in the world. like someone would hold the fork
loaded with the first bite of pancakes
dripping with maple syrup and butter
before they know enough to care about the calories.
Aren't these amazing? and so I look again. more closely.
this is a man who cares about the bits and pieces.
the shards. the cast offs. the broken things of the world.
he spends the days visiting dying patients
and lately, he wonders if he's made any difference at all.
he sees first hand that people have nothing in the end.
except the time they spent doing what they loved
and loving the world the best they could.
all the rest of it. shells.
rubbed and eroded by the sea.
Yes, these are amazing, I say.
and into my cupped hands he places
this treasure.

Willing to Float

The day after solstice. deep winter.
I have a book of exercises about healing grief
by writing poetry. I don't like any of them.
they won't work. not on me. not this time.
I've been looking into the wintry night sky
through a telescope
seeing the vast, endless, emptiness of it all.
the nothingness spackled with stars
that no one can fully explain.
all meaning has been stripped
the way hungry deer pull the tender bark
from the trunks of the sleeping chokecherries.
the only thing I can know for sure
is that when I add hot water
to a packet of ramen noodles
the rigid square of constricted dough
            becomes long, flexible,
            willing
to be wound around a fork many,
many times. willing to float in broth
as salty as a bowl of ocean,
and all it contains—
            from bioluminescent fish
            on its unlit and forgotten floor,
            to phytoplankton steeped in sunlight,
            drifting and wandering along the liquid surface
and suddenly, I am on the beach eating noodles
with my hair blowing loose,
inhaling and exhaling the endless waves.

everything changes. this is how it goes:
            nothing escapes the cold or heat, the grief, the wet,
            the stir of the spoon, the brothy untangling and yet
how much safer it seems to stay dry.
the possible selves I give up
to maintain that dehydrated sensibility.

The Kitchen

I. Ice, A Cube

Sometimes she thaws like a frozen lake
melts in spring. without trying or wanting to.
subject to the sun. the turn of the planet.
the will of the season.
the lake becomes free of the structure imposed
by winter. imposed by her rigid character.
the need for control.
he never washes the dishes correctly.
always dried bits of food
left between the tongs of a fork
or on the outer rims of bowls.
never puts things in their place.
the pots always go in the same cabinet.
doesn't he notice? why doesn't he?
the many years of this.
if she were to soften.
the ease of things.
the constant worry over the many details.
the way they accumulate and end up
as a knot in her stomach.
if she were really ice. a cube.
how wonderful to be plunked into a drink.
slowly dissolve. becoming the beads of sweat
on the sides of the glass.
the coolness and flavor on the tongue.
swallowed by the effortlessness
of thirst.

II. *Down the Drain*

She empties the glass into the sink.
pours out resentment. it flows with the dirty
dish water down the drain.
the large food particles catch in the strainer.
if she is the type of person who examines
the over-sized bits before throwing them out,
she doesn't do that this time. it's like criticism.
a bad habit. unnecessary.
she taps them into the compost
and lets nature take care of it. break it down.
she scrubs the glass. rinses it.
puts it in the dish rack. leaves it there
for the air to dry. maybe, if it's winter,
the sun is streaming through the south facing windows
and it will dry fast. but there is no hurry.
she is in it for the long haul.
this glass is from a set.
a gift at her wedding. 3 of 8 remain.
the years knock chips out of the rims. crack the sides.
sometimes carelessness shatters
the entire thing into shards
that must be hunted down. meticulously.
when she is ready to refill it,
she pays attention to the way it becomes full.
satisfied with that filling. that fullness.
after all these years. some grace
or magic or luck held this glass together yet.
and there is something here she is still
thirsty for.

Attachment Theory

My mother always told me when the guys were no good.
"What are you doing with that idiot? have some self
respect. never be dependent.
make your own way" she always said.
every time I left the house she tried to pin a pair
of butterfly wings on my back
so I could fly strong and certain
on the crazy winds of adolescence.
but I always batted them away.
"Where are you going?" she would yell from the stoop
as we raced out of the house and piled into an old Ford van.
"A party" we yelled over our shoulders.
"Will there be drugs at the party?"
and we always answered "no"
until one day one of us said, "yes"
and she never asked again after that.
maybe she thought I had things figured out
because I acted that way.
no 16 year old is going to admit their shock
at discovering that the world is terrible and horrible and wrong,
with a bit of romantic love mixed in
and that soon they must navigate for themselves.
too soon. but not soon enough.
My mother still can't fathom
how I got into that bassinet
in the room she decorated for me in gold and avocado
with matching curtains and pillows,
how I got a mind full of strange ideas
and a mouth full of poesy.
It is a mystery how we are bound together.
someday (I can't really speak of it)
there will be a time when she disappears
as mysteriously as I appeared in that late 60s décor.
I can't imagine that.
Who will tell me then, what is totally obvious:
he's a jerk. you're being taken advantage of.
take the next step. you can be anything.
don't settle. keep growing.
you are an orange blossom flower
that will bloom forever
even after delicate white petals
are dried and gone.

Metaphor is Litter

I love decadent poetry.
the rich, thick, generous kind.
the kind that transforms me
from this woman worried about deadlines
to this woman ablaze. heart consumed by flame.
coals for words. their hot language my lava speech.
but I'm tired of metaphor. of saying this is that:
loneliness is a razor blade cutting her 16 year old thigh.
love is a GPS that doesn't always get you where you want to go.
the wind is my desire echoing its song of need
in every crevice of the canyon.
everything becomes everything else
in that quest to be carried beyond monotony.
an unbearable tangle of images.
I want things to be themselves.
I want one strand unbound from that mess.
one word that is transparent:
heartbreak.
       exhilaration.
rat.
I don't want to expend energy. uselessly.
just for the sake of appearances. just because I can.
I want to find words that don't need fortification.
find that crux of myself beyond personifications.
Do you understand?
               alive.
      thunder.
web.   *run.*   *stop.*
      hunger.   *bullet.*
water.
laughter.
death.
I keep these words in jars of formaldehyde.
the jars become books. the pages are trees.
the trees were a forest.
cut. milled. bound. littered with my language.
I wipe the black crumb letters off the paper
into my hands. toss them out for Raven.
he only has one word
for all of this excessive human endeavor:

CAW!

Morning Bones

Morning bones are settled,
relaxed, easy, nestled warm
in the blanket of tissue and muscle,
under a cover of skin.
under a down comforter—
where rest thousands of tiny feathers
each with its own central spine
so that even the lightest one
in a weightless dream of levity
has an edifice.

This is the framework upon
which we are formed,
how we structure the day,
how we build a reality
with these solid things.
Then at night
even our bones can be soft, yielding,
regenerate of their own accord.
Until morning
when we jump out of bed
to face the world hard,
harden ourselves into that familiar pattern
and collide into the sureness
of the story we've created
the day before and
the day before.

The Extra Pieces

I gather bones.
arrange the small metacarpals, metatarsals and
phalanges in the silverware tray,
      clean, polish and stack them together
      neatly.
The largest, longest, straightest—
femur, humerus, tibia, ulna
make tools. necessary implements:
      a shovel, a hoe,
      a bat, an umbrella,
and most obviously, a cane.
The oddly shaped bones might be
      for digging (scapula)
      or holding candles (pelvis).
I string the vertebrae as beads,
wear them with a black strapless cocktail dress
at posh parties where people say "Oh. I love your
necklace."
The extra pieces (skull, sternum and ribcage)
become garden art.
I set them so that bright red poppies
grow in the space between ribs
where breath used to expand and release.
      Purple coneflowers emerge from eye sockets
      and teeth are now bright green with tiny moss,
      still smiling here
      in the certainty of decay.

Ready to Enter

Trust the empty spaces.
Let the scaffolding collapse.
Let the collapse be eggplant
sliced thin, breaded,
        sizzling in olive oil
layered with Romano cheese, basil
and marina.
The plate, the table, the
        fork and knife.
The view from the window—
a field of old dandelions
white manes ready
        to enter the open space of the wind,
        to travel and journey around seed
source, source of the moment, the moment
is eating, eating is empty,
in emptiness I'm full.

Trust the dandelions,
the order of shortened days,
        lengthening darkness, rain
        and rusted leaves dropped. Drop
the mind, the image of self as eggplant.
Let hot oil
hiss.

Designed to Catch the Enormous

Always. motion—
each moment a big bang
        filtered by brain,
        its chemicals and fluids,
its electromagnetic charge.
A butterfly net held in the air,
        some of this flying debris
        is caught by awareness.
        Free form
to structure
to language
to lips, they kiss
looking for that space
that emancipation.

Suddenly. ocean.
all syncopates
        with wave and crash,
        the beach pummeled
over and over—
designed to catch the enormous
        spill out,
        of so much water
in motion.
I'm designed. to be fluid
not a bog
not a hurricane—
        a gentle stream
        percolating over the resting rocks
of the Redwood forrest—
held in mossy mouths,
tasted, sated,
simple.

Swirls All

In the wet
of the rain. go.
follow cement until
it is not cement,
is a border place
where leaves rot in piles, stacking
up. Time
creates this. Accumulation.
Items of random assembly:
            a used condom,
            yellow hourglass
(the sand forever clumped in one chamber),
crushed (but unopened) aluminum can, plastic
shards, pennies, a dime, arm
of a doll, busted cinder block, broken
trellis, duck feathers, irrigation tubes.
And unseen stuff
            tucked in. dark places
            I will not reach into.
Rain dislodges
the hidden and hiding,
muddles and swirls all of the bits
and pieces in small
or large puddles.
            twigs, leaves, soil,
            pebbles, yarn, tissues,
cigarette butts, gum wrappers and bottle tops
together make a strange soup—
the growing elements and dead debris
exist simultaneously simmer
inside me
one spoonful
all lost or discarded things
are carried to the sea.

Pulse

One finger on the wrist measures the beat of the heart, the vast
darkness from which it springs.
        Unapparent and under
        the pulse, in the vein
        under the pallid skin,
throbs once, again, alive with liquid red propulsion
like a plump, crimson elderberry
waiting, anticipating, desiring
the delightful and dreaded bite of black bear.
Each berry vibrates with that suspense
as each beat of the bear's heart swells
with the juice of summer fruit.
Devoured and devouring, wanting
and needing, giving and taking,
        this is not about the certainty
        that everything is connected.
        sustained in beauty.
This is about ending, one thing becoming another,
two sides the same—
        hooked, no loss small, each a cumulative weight,
        grief a kind of sustenance for our own living.
The falling of the over-ripe berries
feeds dirt.

Yet at the height of ripeness, luminosity resides in skin,
unassuming moonlight rests on the naked body
        like a white silk kimono lifted in the cool summer breeze.
        The skin like an urn,
        unaware of the coming autumn,
        the decomposition of flesh,
        the drying of inner pulp and juice.

There is no way to avoid the terror
of sharp claws and seeking snout.
of grinding teeth and sucking lips,
there is no way to comprehend
      the ecstasy
      and freedom
      of coursing
through the beating heart of wild creatures—
the fullness of the self
a loosed feather
      in eternity.

You Will Find Yourself

The highway goes on
forever, is the spine of a town, briefly,
then unrolls again like a black licorice rope
into the desert's pebbly landscape.
If you stick out your thumb,
someone might offer you a ride into that
        expanse.
If you walk, your body's thirst
will become large, enormous like the ancient ocean
once sloshing around the now empty belly of valley.
If you sit at the edge of this black line
drawn on the sandy skin of the earth,
you will be a raven,
looking for something shiny
to take home to your nest,
some treasure for your mate and young.

Or you might spread your dark iridescent wings
and lift your body away from gravity,
        float on air currents,
        glide with no effort
as some will that is not your own
pushes you on to L.A.
or further yet into Mexico
and the promise of ocean,
of sea crashing the rocky coastline,
misting you with salty spray and coolness.

In any case,
you will find yourself a traveler
without a suitcase,
only the knowledge of bone and muscle,
heart and blood and wing
guiding you into the sunset
or sunrise.
You will carry like a roadmap
your faith in cycles,
in perpetual motion,
in your own breath—
that great swell of wave
in your lungs.

Renee Podunovich, MA, is a licensed professional counselor and freelance writer. She lives "off the grid" in an Earthship home that she built with her husband in southwest Colorado.

Podunovich's poems were nominated for a Pushcart Prize in 2010 and 2011. Her most recent publications include *Mississippi Review*, *Boston Literary Magazine*, *FutureCycle Poetry*, *Caper Literary Journal*, *White Whale Review*, *The View From Here*, *RATTLE* and *SW Colorado Arts Perspective*.

Her first book of poems *If There Is a Center No One Knows Where It Begins* was published by Art Juice Press in 2008. Writer Cynthia West said of the book, "Podunovich's visions are transparent panes allowing the reader the warmth and light of a larger view. She returns from journeys beyond the daily world with medicine which explodes in us 'with no limits, other than the filter of our hearts'. Her passionate words form conduits through which we can meet our higher selves".

Renee believes that poetry is a language that encourages us to transcend our constricted sense of self and connect to our essential nature within and the spirit of the world around us. Poetry can both express the inner life and bring deeper insight into the mundane.

Renee facilitates poetry workshops that are designed to use creative writing as a tool for centering, reflecting and for personal growth. www.ReneePodunovich.com